The Mindful Hustle

Balancing Ambition and Mental Health in the Age of Burnout

Mike Bhangu

BBP Copyright 2025

Copyright © 2025 by Mike Bhangu.

This book is licensed and is being offered for your personal enjoyment only. It is prohibited for this book to be re-sold, shared and/or to be given away to other people. If you would like to provide and/or share this book with someone else, please purchase an additional copy. If you did not personally purchase this book for your own personal enjoyment and are reading it, please respect the hard work of this author and purchase a copy for yourself.

All rights reserved. No part of this book may be used or reproduced or transmitted in any manner whatsoever without written permission from the author, except for the inclusion of brief quotations in reviews, articles, and recommendations. Thank you for honoring this.

_____

Published by BB Productions
British Columbia, Canada
thinkingmanmike@gmail.com

The Mindful Hustle

Balancing Ambition and Mental Health in the Age of Burnout

Table of Contents

Chapter Outline

Introduction: The Paradox of Modern Ambition

Chapter 1: The Science of Burnout

Chapter 2: Redefining Ambition

Chapter 3: The Daily Grind, Reimagined

Chapter 4: Resilience Through Mindfulness

Chapter 5: The Long Game

Conclusion: The Art of Thriving

Chapter Outline

Introduction: The Paradox of Modern Ambition

- Overview of the cultural obsession with "hustle" and its consequences.

- Introduction to the book's thesis: Sustainable success requires balancing achievement with mental well-being.

- Brief preview of neuroscience, storytelling, and practical strategies as core pillars.

Chapter 1: The Science of Burnout

Understanding Why We Crash

- **1.1:** The Neuroscience of Stress: How chronic ambition impacts the brain (e.g., cortisol, prefrontal cortex dysfunction).

- **1.2:** Cultural Catalysts: Social media, gig economy, and glorification of overwork.

- **1.3:** Real-Life Stories: Profiles of high achievers who hit breaking points.

- **1.4:** Actionable Strategies:** Early warning signs of burnout + "stress audit" exercises.

Chapter 2: Redefining Ambition

Aligning Goals with Well-Being

- **2.1:** Values-Based Success: How to separate ego-driven goals from purposeful ambition.

- **2.2:** Neuroscience of Motivation: Dopamine, reward systems, and sustainable drive.

- **2.3:** Real-Life Stories:** Entrepreneurs/artists who redesigned their definitions of success.
- **2.4:** Actionable Strategies:** Goal-setting frameworks (e.g., SMART goals with mindfulness check-ins).

Chapter 3: The Daily Grind, Reimagined
Building Habits for Sustainable Hustle

- **3.1:** The Power of Micro-Habits: Neuroscience of habit formation (basal ganglia, neuroplasticity).
- **3.2:** Time Management for Humans: Prioritization, rest cycles, and the myth of multitasking.
- **3.3:** Real-Life Stories:** A CEO who adopted a 4-day workweek; a student using "deep work" principles.
- **3.4:** Actionable Strategies:** Time-blocking templates, the "20-5-3" rest rule, and digital detox guides.

Chapter 4: Resilience Through Mindfulness
Training the Mind to Thrive Under Pressure

- **4.1:** Neuroscience of Resilience: How mindfulness strengthens emotional regulation (amygdala, prefrontal cortex).
- **4.2:** Embracing Failure: The growth mindset vs. fixed mindset in high achievers.
- **4.3:** Real-Life Stories:** Athletes/leaders who use meditation, therapy, or creative outlets to cope.
- **4.4:** Actionable Strategies:** 5-minute mindfulness drills, cognitive restructuring exercises, and self-compassion scripts.

Chapter 5: The Long Game

Cultivating Legacy Without Sacrificing Yourself

- **5.1:** Legacy vs. Burnout: How to align daily actions with long-term purpose (neuroscience of meaning: serotonin, oxytocin).

- **5.2:** The Role of Community: Building support systems and delegating effectively.

- **5.3:** Real-Life Stories:** Mentors who model balanced ambition across decades.

- **5.4:** Actionable Strategies:** Quarterly "life audits," creating personal advisory boards, and legacy mapping.

Conclusion: The Art of Thriving

- Recap of key themes: Burnout is not a badge of honor; sustainable success is a practice.

- Call to action: Redefine hustle as mindful, intentional progress.

- Final encouragement to prioritize well-being as the foundation of achievement.

Introduction: The Paradox of Modern Ambition

Welcome to the Cult of Busy

Let's begin with a confession: You're here because you're tired. Not "I-need-a-nap" tired. Not even "I-accidentally-drank-decaf" tired. You're *soul-crushingly, eye-twitchingly, why-is-my-Apple-Watch-judging-me-for-not-standing-up* tired. You're a card-carrying member of the Cult of Busy, where exhaustion is a status symbol and "sleep" is a four-letter word.

But hey, congratulations! You've mastered the art of glorified self-destruction. You can grind a 14-hour workday, meal-prep quinoa in a blender, and reply to emails while pretending to listen to your partner's story about their coworker's cat. You've optimized your life like a Tesla on autopilot—except instead of cruising toward renewable energy, you're hurtling toward a mental breakdown dressed up as a "personal brand."

Welcome to *The Mindful Hustle*, the book that's here to gently pry the cold brew out of your death grip and ask: *"What if success didn't have to feel like a hostage situation?"*

The Great Ambition Paradox

Here's the deal: Society has gaslit us into believing that ambition and well-being are archenemies, like pineapple on pizza or cats and water. We're told to "rise and grind" but also "namaste." To "crush our goals" but also "listen to our bodies." To "network like a boss" but also "touch grass." It's exhausting, confusing, and frankly, bad branding.

The result? We're all stuck in a **Productivity Horror Movie**, playing dual roles as the hero *and* the villain. We chase success like it's the last chopper out of 'Nam, only to realize we're holding the grenade. Burnout isn't just *likely*—it's practically a rite of passage. We wear it like a badge of honor, bragging about our sleepless nights as if they're Boy Scout merit badges. *"Look at me, Karen from HR! I haven't seen sunlight since 2019! I'm basically a vampire, but with worse benefits!"* But here's the twist: **Burnout isn't a flex. It's a failure of imagination.** A failure to ask: *What if we could achieve greatness without treating our mental health like a subscription service we forgot to cancel?*

Why This Book Isn't a TED Talk (Thank God)

This isn't a self-help book written by a guru who levitates while reciting affirmations. (Though if you *can* levitate, please DM me—I have questions.) This is a survival guide for the chronically overcommitted, the recovering perfectionists, and anyone who's ever cried in a Zoom bathroom.

We'll tackle this mess with three weapons:

1. **Neuroscience**: Because nothing says "chill out" like explaining cortisol with PowerPoints.
2. **Real-Life Stories**: Featuring people who've face-planted in the pursuit of success, so you don't have to. (Looking at you, "Dave," who tried to outsource sleep to a meditation app.)
3. **Actionable Strategies**: Including "How to Say 'No' Without Apologizing Like You Ran Over Their Dog" and "Why 'Hustle Porn' is Worse Than Actual Porn."

The Roadmap: From Hot Mess to (Slightly Less Hot) Mess

Here's what you're signing up for:

- **Chapter 1**: We'll dissect why your brain thinks deadlines are lions. Spoiler: Your amygdala is a drama queen.

- **Chapter 2**: How to want success without wanting to flee the country and start a llama farm.

- **Chapter 3**: Time management hacks for people who think "Deep Work" is a Napolean Dynamite sequel.

- **Chapter 4**: Mindfulness: It's not just for people who wear linen pants.

- **Chapter 5**: Building a legacy that doesn't require sacrificing your kneecaps to the Corporate Overlords.

By the end, you'll have a game plan to hustle smarter, not harder—or at least hustle without developing a nervous tic every time your phone buzzes.

A Quick Note Before We Dive In

This book is not a judgment. I've been you. I've cried in office bathrooms. I've powered through flu symptoms to hit a deadline, only to realize the deadline was self-imposed and my boss was on vacation. I've confused burnout for ambition and panic attacks for passion.

But here's the good news: **You don't have to choose between success and sanity.** You can want greatness *and* naps. You can chase big dreams *and* binge Netflix without guilt. You can be ambitious *and* eat a snack that isn't labeled "protein-packed."

The modern hustle is a marathon, not a sprint—and this book is your permission slip to pace yourself.

Ambition shouldn't feel like a Saw movie. Let's fix this.

Chapter 1: The Science of Burnout

Understanding Why We Crash (And How to Stop Resurrecting Like a Low-Budget Horror Movie Villain)

1.1 The Neuroscience of Stress: Or, Why Your Brain Thinks You're Being Chased by a Lion (Spoiler: You're Not)

Let's start with a fun fact: your brain is *dramatic*. Like, *reality-TV-level* dramatic. When you're stressed, it releases cortisol, a hormone that essentially turns your body into a panic room. Cortisol's job is to prep you for danger—say, sprinting away from a saber-toothed tiger. But here's the kicker: **your brain can't tell the difference between a tiger and a Slack notification from your boss at 11 p.m.**

Picture this: You're binge-working on a project, guzzling cold brew like it's the elixir of immortality. Cortisol floods your system. Your prefrontal cortex—the part of your brain that handles logic and decision-making—shuts down like a Walmart on Thanksgiving. Suddenly, you're making choices that would embarrass a raccoon in a dumpster. *"Should I eat this third gas-station taquito? YES. Should I reply 'LOL' to that passive-aggressive email from accounting? ABSOLUTELY."*

Meanwhile, your amygdala (the brain's "sky is falling!" alarm) hijacks the controls. You're now in fight-or-flight mode, except the only thing you're fighting is the urge to cry into your keyboard. Congratulations! You've achieved **"Productive Panic"**—a state where you're technically getting things done, but your nervous system thinks it's starring in *Mad Max: Fury Road*.

1.2 Cultural Catalysts: How Society Gaslit Us Into Thinking Sleep is for the Weak

Let's blame things! Because nothing says "self-care" like pointing fingers. Modern burnout isn't just your brain being extra—it's the lovechild of three toxic trends:

1. **Social Media's "Rise and Grind" Propaganda**: Instagram influencers peddling 4 a.m. routines while posing in athleisure like they're auditioning for *Ocean's 14: Yoga Heist*. Newsflash: If your morning routine involves kale smoothies, journaling, and a 10K run before sunrise, you're either a superhero or a sociopath.

2. **The Gig Economy**: Where "hustle culture" means working seven jobs just to afford avocado toast and a studio apartment the size of a Tesla. You're now a CEO (of your side hustle), a DoorDasher, a TikTok influencer, and a person who occasionally showers. Your résumé looks like a Mad Lib, and your circadian rhythm looks like a Jackson Pollock painting.

3. **Corporate Stockholm Syndrome**: Companies that preach "work-life balance" while emailing you at midnight with "URGENT: Fix the font on Slide 12." They've convinced us that burnout is a *badge of honor*, like surviving a hazing ritual. *"You slept under your desk? Here's a 'Wellness Wednesday' webinar!"*

1.3 Real-Life Stories: When "Hustle" Meets "Hurl"

Meet **"Dave"** (name changed to protect the guilty). Dave was a startup founder who believed sleep was a myth invented by Big Mattress. He worked 20-hour days, fueled by Red Bull and a crippling fear of mediocrity. Then, one fateful Tuesday, Dave's body staged a mutiny.

Mid-pitch to investors, he hallucinated that the conference room plant was Elon Musk. He tried to sell it Tesla stock.

Or **"Karen"** (not her real name, because she's still recovering). Karen was a lawyer who billed 80 hours a week while "mom-ing" two toddlers and training for a marathon. Her breaking point? She showed up to court wearing one high heel and one Croc. The judge asked if it was a new trend. She burst into tears and quoted *The Little Engine That Could* in her closing argument.

These aren't anomalies—they're cautionary tales written in caffeine stains and existential dread.

1.4 Actionable Strategies: How to Stop the Madness (Without Moving to a Yurt)

Time to adult! Here's your **"Burnout First-Aid Kit"**:

1. **The "Am I Dying or Just Overworked?" Checklist**:
    - Are your eye twitches syncing to the beat of your Apple Watch "Stand" reminders?
    - Have you mistaken your coffee cup for a family member?
    - Does the phrase "self-care" make you want to throw your phone into the ocean?
      If you answered "yes" to any of these, congrats! You're in the burnout danger zone.
2. **The Stress Audit™**: A fancy term for "sit down and ask yourself why you're like this."
    - Track your stress triggers for a week. Spoiler: 90% will be emails that could've been a text.

- Rank tasks by "Does this matter?" and "Will I care in 5 years?" Pro tip: Fixating on PowerPoint animations = not a legacy.

3. **The "Doom Scroll Detox"**:
    - Step 1: Delete LinkedIn. (Just kidding! …Unless?)
    - Step 2: Set app limits. When TikTok suggests "5-minute ab workouts," your brain hears "5-minute existential crises."
    - Step 3: Replace one stress habit with something that doesn't involve screens. Try yelling into a pillow. It's free therapy!

4. **The "Cortisol Fire Drill"**: When stress hits, ask: *"Is this a lion? Or just my ego?"* Then breathe like you're inflating a pool floatie. Inhale for 4 counts, exhale for 6. Repeat until you no longer want to fight your Wi-Fi router.

Your brain is a drama queen, society is a bad influencer, and burnout is not a personality trait. To avoid becoming a cautionary LinkedIn post: **Stop treating your body like a rented mule.** Next chapter: How to want success without wanting to yeet yourself into the sun.

Chapter 2: Redefining Ambition

Because "World Domination" Sounds Exhausting (And You're All Out of Henchmen)

2.1 Values-Based Success: Or, How to Stop Chasing Clout Like a Golden Retriever Chasing a Laser Pointer

Let's play a game: *Is This Goal Ego or Soul?*

- **Ego Goal**: "I need to become CEO by 30 so my high school bully cries into his expired gym membership."
- **Soul Goal**: "I want to build something that makes people say, 'Wow, that's neat,' instead of 'Wow, that guy needs therapy.'"

Ambition isn't the problem—it's the *why* behind it. Ego-driven goals are like collecting rare sneakers but never wearing them because you're too busy Instagramming them next to a sad kale salad. They're flashy, hollow, and usually end with you yelling at a barista for spelling your name wrong on a cup that'll be trash in 10 minutes.

Values-based success, on the other hand, is like adopting a rescue dog: messy, meaningful, and occasionally covered in drool. It's about aligning your hustle with what *actually* matters—like leaving the world slightly better than you found it, or at least not leaving your coworkers' group chat on "read" during a mental health day.

2.2 The Neuroscience of Motivation: Dopamine, the Drug We're All Secretly Binge-Using

Your brain runs on dopamine, the same chemical that makes puppies adorable and TikTok addictive. Every time you hit a goal, dopamine hits you back like a high-five from a caffeinated cheerleader. But here's the catch: **Your brain is a dopamine junkie**. It'll chase that high whether you're curing cancer or refreshing LinkedIn for likes like a middle-aged mom at a Zumba class.

The problem? Chasing external validation is like playing a dopamine slot machine. You pull the lever (send the email, post the selfie, binge-work until 3 a.m.), and sometimes you "win" (a promotion, 200 likes, a stress-induced shingles outbreak). But mostly, you lose, and your brain just *keeps pulling*.

Sustainable drive is about rewiring that slot machine into a *vending machine*. Instead of gambling for random rewards, you stock it with what actually fuels you: purpose, curiosity, and snacks. (Seriously, eat a Snickers. You're not you when you're hangry.)

2.3 Real-Life Stories: From Burnout to "Wait, Why Am I Doing This Again?"

Meet **"Tyler"**, a former tech bro who thought "success" meant owning a Tesla, a rooftop hot tub, and a soul-crushing fear of free time. Then he read a self-help book during a panic attack in a Costco parking lot. Today, Tyler runs a llama farm in Vermont. His biggest achievement? "Getting a llama to stop spitting in my coffee. It's like negotiating with a toddler in a fur coat."

Or **"Priya"**, a corporate lawyer who billed 2,500 hours a year while mainlining matcha lattes. Her wake-up call? She won a big case… and celebrated by crying into her desk plant for 45 minutes. Now she's a stand-up comedian who bombs nightly but sleeps like a baby. "Turns out," she says, "laughter *is* the best medicine. Especially when the audience is laughing *at* you."

These folks didn't "give up"—they upgraded their ambitions from "impressing strangers" to "not dying inside."

2.4 Actionable Strategies: How to Want Stuff Without Losing Your Mind (or Your Netflix Password)

Strategy 1: The "SMART-ASS" Goal Framework

Forget SMART goals. Let's get SMART-ASS:

- **Specific**: "I will write 500 words a day" vs. "I will vaguely 'be productive' while staring at my ceiling fan."
- **Meaningful**: Ask, "Does this matter, or did LinkedIn convince me it does?"
- **Aligned**: Does this goal vibe with your values, or is it just your ego doing parkour?
- **Realistic**: "I'll learn Spanish in a month" is code for "I'll panic-Duolingo at the airport."
- **Time-Bound**: Set a deadline. And no, "someday" isn't a day of the week.
- **And Seriously, Sleep**: If your goal requires IV caffeine, it's a bad goal.

Strategy 2: The Dopamine Detox (a.k.a. "Nap Time for Adults")

- Step 1: Delete apps that turn you into a thumb-scrolling zombie (looking at you, TikTok).
- Step 2: Replace one "achievement hit" (e.g., grinding for likes) with a *joy hit* (e.g., petting a dog, baking cookies, watching *Die Hard* for the 90th time).

- Step 3: Brag about your detox. "I didn't check email for 3 hours! My productivity is *evolving*."

Strategy 3: The "Funeral Test"

Ask: *"At my funeral, will anyone care about this goal?"* If the answer is "No, but they'll definitely roast me for that time I cried over a PowerPoint," maybe reprioritize.

Ambition isn't evil—it's just confused. Stop letting your ego drive the Tesla. Align your goals with your soul (or at least a decent nap schedule). And remember: **You're not a robot. Unless you are. In which case, please share your software updates.**

Chapter 3: The Daily Grind, Reimagined

How to Work Like a Human, Not a Roomba with a LinkedIn Account

3.1 The Power of Micro-Habits: Or, How Your Brain Became a Couch Potato

Your brain's basal ganglia is that friend who still wears sweatpants from 2012 and thinks "meal prep" is ordering two pizzas instead of one. It *loves* habits—the lazier, the better. Every time you mindlessly scroll Instagram at 2 a.m. or stress-eat Oreos during Zoom calls, your basal ganglia high-fives itself like it just won the lottery. *"Look at us! We're efficient!"*

But here's the secret: **Neuroplasticity means your brain is as moldable as Play-Doh left in the sun**. You *can* teach it new tricks—like swapping "doomscrolling" for "literally anything else." Start small. Micro-habits are the LEGO bricks of adulthood. Floss one tooth. Drink one sip of water. Reply to one email without typing "ASAP" in all caps. Baby steps! Or as your basal ganglia calls it: *"Ugh, fine, but I'm not happy about it."*

3.2 Time Management for Humans: Because Robots Don't Need Snack Breaks

Let's debunk the **Big Lie of Multitasking**: You're not a superhero. You're a person trying to juggle chainsaws while riding a unicycle on a tightrope. Spoiler: *The chainsaws are on fire, and the unicycle is a metaphor for your mental health.*

Prioritization 101:

- **Urgent vs. Important**: Urgent = "My boss is texting." Important = "My therapist is texting."

- **The 80/20 Rule**: 20% of your efforts cause 80% of your results. The other 80% is you reorganizing your Spotify playlists to "optimize focus."

- **Rest Cycles**: Your brain isn't a Tesla battery. It needs breaks. Try the **"20-5-3" Rule**:
    - *20 minutes* of work.
    - *5 minutes* of staring at a wall questioning your life choices.
    - *3 deep breaths* so you don't strangle the next person who says "synergy."

3.3 Real-Life Stories: From Chaos to "Meh, Good Enough"

Meet **"Janelle"**, a CEO who once believed "sleep is for the weak" until she hallucinated a board meeting in her shower. She switched to a 4-day workweek and—plot twist—*productivity skyrocketed.* Her team now uses Fridays for "innovation," which is corporate code for "napping at desks with Slack status set to 'In a meeting.'"

Then there's **"Carlos"**, a college student who treated studying like a WWE match: chaotic, loud, and ending with a cram session so intense he once wrote an essay on Kafka… in Klingon. After adopting "deep work" (read: turning off TikTok), he aced his finals. His secret? "I stopped pretending Wikipedia tabs count as 'research.'"

3.4 Actionable Strategies: How to Adult Without Losing Your Marbles

Strategy 1: Time-Blocking for the Chronically Distracted
- **Step 1**: Divide your day into chunks. Example:
  - *9-10 a.m.*: "Strategic Coffee Procurement" (i.e., staring into the abyss of your Keurig).
  - *10-12 p.m.*: "Pretending to Work While Actually Googling 'Can stress cause toenails to fall off?'"
- **Step 2**: Use apps to block distractions. Pro tip: If you block Netflix, *actually block it*. "Just one episode" turns into "Why is the sun rising?"

Strategy 2: The "Unsubscribe from Life" Detox
- **Digital Detox**: Delete apps that suck your soul. If you wouldn't let a vampire into your house, why let TikTok into your brain?
- **Email Bankruptcy**: Declare inbox bankruptcy. Mass-delete everything older than a week. If it was important, they'll follow up. If not, *congrats—you've cured their procrastination too!*

Strategy 3: The "Snack-Based Productivity System"
- Assign tasks to snacks. Finish a report? Eat a gummy bear. Hit a deadline? Crush a granola bar like Thor's hammer.
- Warning: Do not attempt this with kale chips. Nobody needs that kind of negativity.

Your brain is a lazy roommate, multitasking is a scam, and rest is not a crime. Hack your habits, block your time, and *for the love of god, stop Googling your symptoms.*

Chapter 4: Resilience Through Mindfulness

Training the Mind to Thrive Under Pressure (Without Becoming a Crystal-Hugging Hippie)

4.1 The Neuroscience of Resilience: Or, How to Stop Your Amygdala from Scream-Singing "All by Myself"

Your amygdala is that friend who texts "OMG CALL ME RN" at 3 a.m. only to say they saw a spider. It's your brain's panic button, wired to interpret *everything* as a crisis—deadlines, spilled coffee, accidentally liking your ex's LinkedIn post from 2017. But here's the kicker: **mindfulness is like slapping a "Chill the Heck Out" sticker on that panic button**.

When you practice mindfulness, you're basically giving your prefrontal cortex—the brain's "adult in the room"—a megaphone to shout over your amygdala's karaoke rendition of *Stress Anthem*. Studies show mindfulness thickens your prefrontal cortex, making it better at saying, "Karen, the printer jam isn't a five-alarm fire. Breathe. Or at least stop crying into the paper tray."

Think of it as mental CrossFit. You're not trying to levitate or "manifest vibes"; you're bench-pressing your attention span back from TikTok oblivion.

4.2 Embracing Failure: Or, Why Falling on Your Face is the New Glow-Up

Let's get real: Failure sucks. But refusing to fail is like refusing to pee—eventually, you'll explode in a messy, public way. High achievers often treat failure like a bad Tinder date: *swipe left, pretend it never happened, rinse with shame.* But **resilience isn't about avoiding faceplants; it's about learning to faceplant** *gracefully*.

Enter the **Growth Mindset vs. Fixed Mindset Smackdown**:

- **Fixed Mindset**: Believes talent is innate. Fails once? *"I'm a trash goblin. Time to binge Bridgerton and eat frosting straight from the can."*
- **Growth Mindset**: Believes skills are built. Fails once? *"Cool, now I know what not to do. Also, frosting is a valid coping mechanism."*

The key difference? One sees failure as a funeral; the other sees it as a *feedback loop* (with snacks).

4.3 Real-Life Stories: From Panic Attacks to "Namaste, Drama"

Meet "**Nina**", a Fortune 500 exec who used to treat panic attacks like coffee breaks—frequent, jittery, and followed by existential dread. Her turning point? She tried meditating during a board meeting. *"I opened Zoom, muted myself, and did breathwork while they argued about Q3 metrics. By minute five, I realized I'd rather be unemployed than unhinged."* Now she teaches "Mindful Mondays" at her company. Participation is optional, but HR *strongly suggests it*.

Or "**Jared**", a pro athlete who blew a championship game by tripping over his own shoelaces. His 15-second viral shame spiral? *"I cried, bought a parrot, and named it 'Karma.'"* Therapy and mindfulness turned him into a resilience coach. His motto: *"If you're not failing, you're not trying to fail enough."*

4.4 Actionable Strategies: How to Zen Out Without Selling Your Soul to a Yoga Studio

Strategy 1: The "5-Minute Mental Fire Drill"

- **Step 1**: When stress hits, ask: *"Is this a real problem or a Twitter problem?"* (Pro tip: If it involves Elon Musk, it's probably both.)

- **Step 2**: Breathe like you're blowing up a pool floatie. Inhale for 4 counts, exhale for 6. Repeat until your amygdala stops quoting *The Hunger Games*.

- **Step 3**: Chug water. Dehydration makes everything worse, like a hangover without the fun pregame.

Strategy 2: The "Failure Debrief" (a.k.a. Post-Mortem Without the Corpse)

After a screw-up, ask:

1. *"What did I learn? (Besides 'never trust a PDF named 'FINAL_FINAL_v2'?)"*

2. *"Would I judge a friend for this?"* (Hint: No. You'd buy them wine and meme about it.)

3. *"What's one tiny win?"* (Example: *"I didn't set anything on fire. Growth!"*)

Strategy 3: The "Lazy Person's Meditation"

- **Option A**: Stare at a wall for 2 minutes and call it "mindfulness." (Bonus: Name the wall "Steve." Bonding!)

- **Option B**: Walk somewhere without headphones. Let your brain marinate in silence. Warning: May cause sudden clarity.

- **Option C**: Chew a raisin like it's a $500 truffle. *"Wow, texture! Existential dread? Never heard of her."*

Strategy 4: The "Self-Compassion Script"

Replace self-criticism with lines you'd use on a toddler:

- *"You tried your best, and that's enough!"*
- *"Oopsie! Let's try again after juice boxes."*
- *"No, sweetie, you're not terrible—you're learning!"*

Your brain's drama can be downgraded from Broadway to community theater. Mindfulness isn't about om-ing; it's about *unclenching*. Failures are plot twists, not tragedies. And yes, you *can* meditate without buying bamboo socks.

Chapter 5: The Long Game

Cultivating Legacy Without Sacrificing Yourself (Or Turning Into a Cryptkeeper)

5.1 Legacy vs. Burnout: Or, How to Avoid Being Remembered as "That Workaholic Who Yelled at a Barista"

Let's talk legacy. You know, that thing you're supposedly building while surviving on protein bars and existential dread? Most of us treat legacy like a Netflix series: *We want 10 seasons, but we're burning out by Season 2.*

Neuroscience of Meaning: Your brain runs on two key chemicals when it comes to fulfillment:

- **Serotonin**: The "happiness intern" that shows up when you feel valued.
- **Oxytocin**: The "cuddle hormone" that spikes when you bond with humans who aren't just Slack avatars.

Problem is, the modern hustle replaces these with cortisol and caffeine, turning your brain into a *Breaking Bad* meth lab of stress. Building a legacy isn't about cramming achievements into a resume like you're stuffing a suitcase for a guilt trip. It's about aligning your daily grind with what makes you whisper, *"Damn, that mattered."*

Think of it this way: **Legacy is a garden, not a dumpster fire**. Tend it with care, or you'll spend retirement explaining to your grandkids why "burnout" is your middle name.

5.2 The Role of Community: Because Even Batman Needs Alfred (and a Decent Wi-Fi Password)

Newsflash: You're not a solo act. You're a *collaborative disaster* in need of backup dancers. Yet high achievers often treat asking for help like admitting they don't know the Wi-Fi password. *"I'll just... figure it out. Googles 'How to build a rocket alone'."*

Delegation 101:

- **Step 1**: Acknowledge you're not a Swiss Army knife. You're a spoon. A *very tired* spoon.

- **Step 2**: Find your "Alfreds" (the competent ones) and your "Penguins" (the ones who'll accidentally email the CEO your cat memes).

- **Step 3**: Trust people to handle things. Yes, even if their first draft looks like it was written by a raccoon on Red Bull.

Community-Building Pro Tips:

- Join groups that don't involve networking. *"Sorry, Karen, my book club only reads Garfield comics."*

- Swap "transactional" relationships for *"Hey, wanna vent over tacos?"* bonds.

- Remember: Your legacy isn't just what you do—it's who you *lift up* while doing it. (Unless you're a CEO. Then it's also who you *laid off*.)

5.3 Real-Life Stories: From Zombie CEOs to "Actually, I Have a Life" Legends

Meet **"Greg"**, a startup founder who once believed "teamwork" meant doing everything himself while his employees watched in horror. His wake-up call? He coded for 72 hours straight and tried to pitch investors in a bathrobe. *"They said no, but they did offer me a Xanax."* Now Greg runs a co-op where decisions are made by committee... and *snack votes*. Or **"Lena"**, a surgeon who treated her personal life like an appendix—useless and optional. After her third divorce (to a man she'd nicknamed "What's-His-Name"), she started mentoring med students. *"Turns out, teaching someone to suture is way more fulfilling than arguing about whose turn it was to buy toilet paper."*

5.4 Actionable Strategies: How to Not Die Before Your Wikipedia Page Does

Strategy 1: The "LEGACY" Checklist

- Leave work at work (or at least stop emailing from the bathroom).
- Embrace "good enough" over "perfect" (your eulogy won't mention PowerPoint fonts).
- Get a hobby that isn't "stress-baking at 2 a.m."
- Ask for help (yes, even if it means admitting you're lost).
- Cultivate *one* relationship that doesn't involve a Zoom link.
- Yell "NO" to things that don't spark joy (or at least mild interest).

Strategy 2: The "Delegate Like You're Dying" Drill

- Write down every task you hate. Now, outsource *one*.
- Pro tip: If you delegate to a colleague, bribe them with snacks. If you delegate to a robot, pray it doesn't gain sentience.

Strategy 3: The "Community Vibe Check"

- Audit your inner circle. Keep the ones who'd bail you out of jail. Ditch the ones who'd post your mugshot.

- Host a *non-work* event. Example: "Bad Movie Night" where you roast *Sharknado* and pretend you're not checking emails.

Strategy 4: The "Quarterly Life Audit"

- Every 3 months, ask:

    1. *"Am I closer to my legacy or just my boss's bonus?"*
    2. *"Would my younger self high-five me or file a restraining order?"*
    3. *"Have I hugged someone this week who isn't a pet or a potted plant?"*

Legacy isn't a trophy—it's a vibe. Build it with humans, not hustle. Delegate like your sanity depends on it (it does). And remember: **Nobody's tombstone says, "Here lies Karen. She nailed Q4."**

Conclusion: The Art of Thriving

Or, How to Finally Stop Impersonating a Sock Puppet of Productivity

The Grand Finale: Burnout is *Not* a Participation Trophy
Let's recap: You've spent years sprinting through life like it's a Black Friday sale, elbowing past sanity and sleep to grab the last discounted TV of "success." But here's the twist: **Life isn't a sprint. It's a marathon where the hydration stations serve margaritas and the finish line is a hammock.**

This book wasn't about quitting hustle. It was about *upgrading* hustle. Trading "grind 'til you're ground beef" for "work smart, nap smarter." You've learned that cortisol is a drama queen, dopamine is a needy ex, and your amygdala really needs a Xanax. But the real takeaway? **You're not a machine. You're a human with Wi-Fi and a questionable Spotify playlist.**

- **Burnout**: Not a personality trait. More like a "check engine" light for your soul.
- **Ambition**: Best served with a side of "chill the heck out."
- **Mindfulness**: Less "om," more "oh, maybe I *shouldn't* email my boss at 3 a.m."
- **Legacy**: What you leave behind when you're not busy LinkedIn-bragging about your 80-hour workweek.

Your Permission Slip to Adult Differently

Go forth, dear reader, and *thrive*. But let's define "thriving" as:

- Working hard, then harder at *not* working.
- Chasing goals like a golden retriever chases tennis balls—*with joy*, not existential dread.
- Treating rest like a VIP guest, not a door-to-door salesman you pretend not to hear.

Remember:

- If your to-do list doesn't include "existential staring," you're doing it wrong.
- Failure is just the universe's way of saying, "Plot twist!"
- And yes, *you can want greatness and also want a snack.*

A Final Note from Your Friendly Neighborhood Burnout Survivor

I wrote this book because I once cried over a PowerPoint. *Twice.* I treated "self-care" like a tax evasion scheme and "work-life balance" like a mythical creature. But here's what I learned: **You don't have to set yourself on fire to keep others warm.**

So unclench your jaw. Delete the productivity apps that guilt-trip you. And the next time someone says, "You can sleep when you're dead," reply: *"Cool, but I'd rather not look like a zombie at my own funeral."*

The Last Laugh

Life's too short to be the star of your own productivity horror movie. So mute the notifications, redefine "hustle," and remember: **The most powerful thing you can achieve is a life that doesn't require a recovery playlist.**

Now go eat a snack. Preferably one that isn't labeled "protein-packed."

Hustle smart, nap hard, and remember: You're not a robot. (Unless you are. In which case, please share your software updates.)

The End

(Or as I like to call it: "The Start of Your Midlife Crisis-Free Era.")

P.S. If you enjoyed this book, leave a review. If you hated it, blame my amygdala. It's dramatic like that.

www.ingramcontent.com/pod-product-compliance
Lightning Source LLC
Chambersburg PA
CBHW070804040426
42333CB00061B/2450